NLP for beginners

Step by step to more success with simple psychology, manipulation techniques and the right body language

Boris Lehmann

CONTENTS

Foreword

Do you want to learn how to effectively manipulate other people? This book aims to be your guide, reference work and companion. People often think that manipulating others is a bad thing. But this does not have to be the case. Consider in advance whether you want to force the person to do something that is not good for them.

If you can answer this question in the negative, what are the arguments against using manipulation techniques? We all unconsciously manipulate other people all the time and are also unconsciously manipulated by others. People who are good manipulators have only learned to do this consciously. We can often even incorporate what the other person wants. Manipulation techniques can therefore help you to deal more ethically with your fellow human beings.

In this book, unlike many other guides on this topic, we will focus primarily on the perspective and techniques of so-called NLP. You will gradually learn what this is and how you can use it in the course of this book. This approach is supported by the fact that NLP is a good, proven and subtle method of manipulating others. It is more difficult for the other person to recognize that they have been manipulated than with some other techniques. With this in mind, I hope you enjoy reading this book!

What is NLP?

NLP is an abbreviation and stands for "neuro-linguistic programming". You may not have much of an idea what this term means. So let's first take a look at the parts that make up this word. This will give you an idea of what NLP is all about.

The **N** stands for "Neuro". You may be familiar with the term from neurology - the medical science of the human nervous system. More generally, the abbreviation "neuro" is used to introduce many terms relating to the nervous system or the psyche. In the case of NLP, the N stands for the fact that this method aims to achieve long-term changes in a person's psyche, some of which can be explained by biological or nervous processes.

The **L** stands for "linguistic". Linguistics is the general science of language. NLP increasingly uses verbal and non-verbal communication techniques to influence other people.

The **P** in NLP is particularly interesting: it stands for "program". You may associate this less with people than with computers and other technology. However, NLP uses the basic psychological assumption that people can be "programmed" by another person. Just as a computer can be made to do certain things by a corresponding program, this can also be achieved with people.

In summary, NLP is a method of using communication techniques to change people's behavior. NLP originates primarily from more recent psychotherapeutic approaches and is used by many therapists in the treatment of mentally ill people. NLP is easy to learn and can therefore also be used by non-professionals. With the help of NLP, you can learn to penetrate the subconscious of other people and thus "control" them. Of course, there are limits to this. You should not expect to be able to take complete control over others through NLP. Nevertheless, you will be amazed at what is possible with NLP!

THE HISTORY OF THE DEVELOPMENT OF NLP

In order to understand how this rather unusual method came into being, you should take a look at the developers and the research history behind this technique. Even if you want to put it into practice as quickly as possible: Take time to understand the theoretical backbone of NLP, then you will find it easier to apply the methods described and really understand what you are doing when you use NLP in your everyday life. NLP is a young discipline that was only developed in the 1970s. In the 1960s, a movement called the Human Potential Movement emerged in the USA. This movement was based on the assumption that every person has great untapped potential and that developing this potential not only leads to a higher quality of life, but also to more serenity and emotional strength and therefore promises a more fulfilling life.

The impressions that a person gathers in the course of their life, their experiences and how they perceive them, all of this determines the formation of character, defines a person just as much as it can set limits for them. A decisive factor in overcoming one's own limitations - one of the most important prerequisites for achieving the goals of NLP - is a better understanding of what remains unknown to many throughout their lives - their own subconscious. The part of our mind that we cannot actively access, but which plays a major role in the perception and processing of experiences.

A look at the founders reveals how the combination of psychology, linguistics and the idea of programming people came about. NLP was developed by two men who initially seemed to be quite different: John Grinder was almost 40 years old at the time and a professor at the University of California in Santa Cruz. Grinder studied linguistics and was studying and researching at the University of Santa Cruz at the time.

At the time, Richard Bandler, ten years his junior, was studying a peculiar combination of subjects at the same university: mathematics, information science and psychology. Grinder originally supervised a group therapy session that Bandler conducted with mentally ill people as part of his studies. However, the two got on well and quickly realized that they were both interested in communicative processes in therapeutic settings. So they began to research communication in Bandler's therapy group together. They gradually worked out various communication principles that seemed to work in the group. They were particularly interested in the question of what communicative factors were needed for a patient to successfully complete their therapy. They collected their observations and used them to formulate specific therapeutic and communicative techniques.

This gave rise to the first version of NLP, to which Bandler devoted himself fully after completing his studies. Later, Grinder and Bandler added another aspect to their research, known as modeling. They focused on people who were considered to be particularly successful and distinguished therapists in their respective fields. They then tried to find out what these people did differently from their less successful contemporaries. In this way, they uncovered more and more principles that have found their way into NLP today.

Although Grinder and Bandler attempted to establish NLP as a subject of scientific research from the 1980s onwards, this was only partially successful. Academic schools usually take the view that NLP does not fulfill the criteria of an independent research field. This may be mainly due to the fact that NLP combines various psychotherapeutic approaches and concepts. Not all of these concepts have been able to demonstrate a therapeutic effect in academic studies. For successful manipulation using NLP, however, this fact should not matter to you! Due to the unwillingness of the academic sciences to deal with NLP as a form of therapy to be taken seriously, NLP has increasingly found its way into coaching.

An example: You are dissatisfied with your body, want to change something about it and sign up for a gym. You train intensively and euphorically for the first three months, change your diet and suddenly you fall into a deep hole, stop training and are frustrated because you haven't stuck with it.

What happened? You have lost faith in yourself at this very moment. This is where NLP can help you. The right mindset can help you achieve any goal you set for yourself. You just need to look at your own goals, pave the way and work towards achieving that goal. Everyone has different things they use to motivate themselves. To find these motivational points, you can, for example, talk to people close to you or, in this case, your personal trainer.

If you want to achieve your dream body with defined muscles through intensive training, then you need to have a precise idea of what your well-toned body should look like. How much weight do you want to put on the scales? How visible do you want your muscles to be? By when do you want to have reached your goal? Set yourself a deadline. In order to achieve your goals and wishes, you need to deal with them and visualize them, as this is the only way to achieve your goal.

People have around 60,000 - 80,000 thoughts running through their heads every day. The majority of these thoughts are negative, even if you are not even aware of them. And they manage to make you feel bad. Think about whether the events and situations in your environment cause sadness, anger, fear or nervousness. The answer is clearly no. Why? Well, the way you think and assess this particular constellation has immense power. If they are negative, they are a great burden. One and the same initial situation can be interpreted in very different ways. It is therefore not the actual situation that causes these feelings, but your assessment of it.

A small example: A friend cancels a date with you. Now you may think that your friend has canceled because he is not that interested in you. This thought makes you feel lonely and sad. However, if you think that your friend doesn't have time because he may have forgotten an important date and is sad about having to cancel on you, you don't need to feel sad. You can simply look forward to the next date.

"It's not the things that bother us, but the way we perceive them." Epictetus

THE 11 CORNERSTONES OF NLP

1. Every person lives in their own special, individual way. This also means that they perceive the world in a special, unique way.
2. Our mind, body and environment are in constant interaction. Your actions can influence the way you think. Your thoughts can also affect the way you feel.
3. Our silence is also a form of communication. The reaction of our conversation partner shows the importance of communication.
4. Individual experiences shape each person and give them their very own reality, according to which they act.
5. Offer your counterpart several options or courses of action, as this increases the chance of achieving the desired goal.

6. Every person makes the best choice for themselves based on the possibilities that exist in their reality. This also means that they always behave in the best possible way within the scope of their possibilities.

7. A person's behavior always makes sense in their perception of the world and is the result of a positive intention. No matter how a person behaves, their behavior is always beneficial to them.

8. The necessary possibilities/requirements for change lie within each person themselves.

9. Everyone has the ability to learn new things and change habitual patterns of behavior.

10. There is no failure, only feedback. You were not successful? Try a different method.

11. Flexibility is the key to success.

BASIC ASSUMPTIONS OF NLP

Now that you know roughly where NLP comes from and how it came about, let's look more at the theoretical foundations of the method. It is not necessary for you to understand all the details of the theoretical skeleton of NLP. However, it is good if you are familiar with the basic terms and concepts. This will make it easier for you to understand how the individual techniques work. You will also understand the basics of how the human psyche works. To be able to manipulate successfully, this knowledge is very helpful, if not obligatory, because you can be the best user of manipulation techniques, but manipulating others requires a high degree of flexibility. It requires a constant ability to adapt to situations and ongoing communication processes. Good manipulators are above all masters of the situation.

It is inherent to NLP that the subjective perception of a person is more important than the objective truth. For a person, there is only one subjective truth. Because we are limited to our five senses when it comes to perceiving the world, we cannot know what is objectively true. We therefore rely on our inner assumptions about what is true.

The five senses are therefore accorded a high degree of relevance: they are the decisive clock for our inner truths. To a certain extent, we are able to recognize our inner truths as false, but this ability is very limited. When you program a person neurolinguistically, you therefore try to penetrate their inner self to such an extent that their previous subjective truth is actually overwritten by a new subjective truth. As you can see: This method can be enormously powerful and can change people in a certain direction in the long term!

NLP assumes that each of the five senses represents a separate communication channel that we can address: This refers to the five sensory channels, whereby NLPers speak of **VAKOG**. **V** stands for visual, i.e. to see; **A** for auditory - to hear -, **K** for kinaesthetic - to feel -, **O** for olfactory - to smell -, and finally **G** for gustatory - to taste.

All experiences are perceived via these channels and processed and stored in the corresponding apparatuses, the so-called representational systems, in the brain. All experiences, memories and your current experience take place in these channels and are processed there. You experience and store them as combinations of images, sounds, feelings, smells and tastes. Completely unconsciously, every person uses their representation systems and channels almost every second. We have a certain preference, also unconsciously, as to which systems and channels are used more frequently and preferentially.

Here is a brief example to illustrate this: A director, for example, must necessarily have a strong visual imagination in order to know how he wants to stage which scene in his latest movie. This requires a practiced visual imagination, which you don't have if you prefer the auditory channel. Logically, this plays a more important role for musicians. Composing music requires not only a certain amount of musical talent, but above all a good acoustic imagination that enables you to hear the sounds in your head even without notes or instruments. This ability can be so pronounced that you can hear certain things even if you are deaf - just think of Beethoven, who composed while deaf in his final years.

This mostly unconscious favoring of certain channels and systems can even go so far as to directly influence our use of language. For example, people who tend to use the visual channel often use words that are also directly linked to visual associations. In these cases, the choice of words is representative of the preferred perception variant and also happens unconsciously. In the case of a presentation in a business meeting, for example, a person with a more auditory disposition will say: "That sounds great!", whereas a person with a visual disposition will say: "That looks very good!".

Our inner truth is therefore very strongly limited by our personal constellation of preferred sensory perceptions. At the same time, we are particularly susceptible to changes in our inner truth through precisely these preferred communication channels. So if you want to fundamentally change something in another person, it is best to address them through the channels that they "understand" best. Incidentally, people can be sorted into groups based on their communication preferences. This gives rise to the famous learning types, because we also absorb information most quickly and effectively through our preferred communication channels.

Exercise 1: Find out your preferred perception channels!

There are various ways in which you can find out which senses you prefer to use to perceive things, the simplest of which is language. Your personal way of perception is also reflected in your language!

People who belong to the **visual type** often make statements like the following:

"I don't see a problem ..."

"I can (not/well) imagine that."

"I (don't) see that."

"The meaning of it all is (not) revealed to me."

The **auditory type tends** to make the following statements:

"This idea sounds good/bad."

"I wonder ..."

"I often say to myself ..."

"That's music to my ears."

The **kinaesthetic type** not only relates to their sense of touch, but also attaches importance to feelings and intuition. As a result, this leads to statements like these:

"I have an (un)good feeling about this."

"I sense a problem there."

"I can't quite grasp it."

"My gut tells me ..."

"I shudder at the thought."

"I get cold/hot at the thought."

The **olfactory type** and the **gustatory type** are usually **combined**, as these two senses are strongly interdependent, which can lead to the following or similar statements:

"That really stinks."

"It stinks to high heaven."

"That smells like fraud."

"I can smell that for miles against the wind."
"The idea alone makes me sick."
"I don't like the idea at all."

To find out which type you personally belong to, spend a whole day paying more attention to what you say in conversations. To intensify the exercise, it is advisable to record a longer conversation with a friend, acquaintance or relative - assuming they agree - so that you can then analyze how you express yourself. Alternatively, you can sit down at the end of the day and write down in detail everything that happened that day.

In particular, write down your thoughts and feelings that have arisen as reactions to the experience. Do not pay attention to your expression while writing so as not to distort the result. Only afterwards, when reading through what you have put down on paper, should you take a close look at which forms of expression describe the nature of your perception. A third way to find out what your preferred channels of perception are is to go for a walk. Don't get lost in your thoughts, but make an effort to observe the world around you as consciously as possible. As soon as you get back home, sit down immediately and write down all the impressions that have stuck in your mind. This is probably the most effective way to track down your preferred channels of perception!

NLP TECHNIQUES AND STRATEGIES

Anchoring

Just as dogs can be conditioned to automatically follow certain actions with certain reactions, you can also condition your own psyche to follow a specific stimulus with a specific reaction. This is called anchoring, whereby the reaction in this case is a specific emotion. In contrast to the reflex, a completely unconscious and uncontrollable reaction to a stimulus, anchoring involves consciously conditioning the psyche to automatically associate an emotion with a stimulus.

Everyone has such anchors in their lives, but most of the time they are unconscious. If you close your eyes and take a moment to reflect, some anchors come to mind. For example, a song that you associate with the same emotion every time you hear it. The same can also apply to a movie scene, looking at a painting or a photograph or very trivial everyday objects such as a brand of a very specific car manufacturer. These stimuli can be not only visual, but also acoustic or olfactory in origin. Almost everyone associates some kind of emotion with a meal, such as grandmother's famous potato soup, or the scent of an almost beguiling perfume. All of these are anchors, but the most important and most relevant for neuro-linguistic programming are those that provoke the strongest and most intense emotional states, because NLP can be used to transform negative feelings in response to certain stimuli and replace them with positive ones.

This method is based on Pavlov's concept of classical conditioning, which links back to the dogs mentioned at the beginning. Ivan Petrovich Pavlov was a Russian physician and behavioral scientist who became famous for his research with dogs. In the course of one of these series of experiments, Pavlov rang a bell every time before the dogs were served a meal. This acoustic conditioning, which caused the dogs to associate the sound of the ringing bell with food, ensured that they did not salivate only when they ate, but even when they only heard the sound of the bell.

The same principle can also be applied to humans, for example to link feelings of happiness with a very specific stimulus, a trigger, and to be able to evoke the desired emotion in this way under any circumstances and at any time. It does not matter which stimulus is used to perceive the trigger, whether it is a heard or self-generated sound, a visual signal, an olfactory or a sensitive one. When used correctly, anchoring works with each of the five senses.

Enough theory, here is an exercise for you to do at home: in order to anchor a feeling, you must first trigger it tangibly. For example, if you want to anchor the feeling of joy in yourself, you should think of a situation that gave you a lot of joy.

As you focus on this feeling, you should try to relax. The feeling of pleasure should gradually increase. It is helpful if you visualize the situation in detail. Concentrate on your breathing and close your eyes to get a concrete picture. What did the environment look like when you felt pleasure? What did it smell like? Do you remember a voice speaking at that time? As soon as the feeling inside you becomes stronger, hold on to the sensation and feel it intensely. Feel the joy growing ever greater inside you. At the peak of this feeling, you should set the anchor. This means that you make a certain gesture, say a certain word or touch a certain part of your body.

It is important that your anchor represents something special, so that it cannot be easily confused. This is the only way you can use it later when you want to evoke the feeling of pleasure. When touching it, make sure that it is a place that you do not touch often out of habit, such as your arm. Nevertheless, it is advisable to make sure that you can easily move your anchor point. Now you can test your anchor. Detach yourself from the feeling of pleasure and think about something else. When you are ready, you can release the anchor. If you feel a sense of joy, your anchor has already worked. If this is not the case, you can repeat the method until the desired feeling arises. Sometimes a feeling is already anchored after the first time. However, you may also need several attempts to anchor the desired sensory impression.

Report
Many people are already familiar with this form of the mirror effect - some people are unconsciously affected by it. In principle, it involves people adapting their facial expressions, gestures and general articulation to the other person during a conversation, i.e. adopting certain behavioral patterns. The more sympathetic the conversation partner is perceived to be, the faster this mirroring takes place and the more characteristics are affected. Rapport is to be understood as a kind of relationship in which harmony and mutual acceptance

prevail. If two or more people are in rapport during their communication, they often maintain eye contact and often align their posture and voice. However, this effect can also be reversed - if you consciously mirror certain gestures and expressions of the person you are talking to, you will be perceived more sympathetically by them and build up an interpersonal relationship characterized by positive signals - rapport.

Calibrate

In the context of neurolinguistic programming, the term "calibrating" is a substitute for the terms "calibrating" or "adjusting". This means that the process of communication, which is repeatedly described, is about adapting to the other person and thus perceiving their verbal and non-verbal expression and responding appropriately. "Calibrating a person" makes it possible to know or anticipate the reaction of another person. It also makes it possible to know whether a person is telling the truth or lying. In short, "calibrating" means "perceiving". It is a sensitive, precise, observant and empathetic perception of the behavior, behavioral changes and statements of the interaction partner.

It should also be noted that not only external states, such as verbal expressions and postures of the body, are important, but also and above all the non-verbal signals that a counterpart sends out. As an actor in the context of neurolinguistic programming, you want to use the technique of calibration. First of all, as already mentioned, you should observe and perceive your counterpart intensively. In a second step, however, it is also important that you "calibrate" yourself to your counterpart. This means, for example, that you should pay close attention to how the other person behaves, how they look or speak, and perhaps also how the handshake or hug feels. With the help of this "calibration", you will be able to perceive even tiny changes in the other person's behavior at a later date and interpret them accordingly.

Pacing and leading
Pacing and leading are further techniques that are part of the concept of neuro-linguistic programming. The term "pacing" stands for actively responding to or adjusting to the sensitivities of another person. The term therefore means tuning into or empathizing with the other person's world. Pacing can be used to find ways to empathize with the other person in a special way.

The term "leading" describes the opposite area to sensitive empathy with others. The aim here is to pull other people along with you in your own plans. It therefore means taking on a leading role. The role helps to respond to the sensitivities previously perceived in pacing, to help the person and to change their experience. It can therefore be said that pacing is a kind of prerequisite for carrying out leading and thus being able to ensure processes of change.

Six-step reframing

This is perhaps the most famous of all NLP models for changing unloved or detrimental habits and behavioral patterns. As the name suggests, this is done using a six-step plan.

Six-step reframing is particularly suitable for psychosomatic disorders and those behavioral patterns that do not occur consciously but unconsciously and are therefore difficult to grasp and understand. The first step is primarily about identifying the trait that you want to change, making it clear to yourself that this trait is causing you problems and setting yourself the clear goal of changing it.

So first of all, you need to understand who you are deep down inside. Be clear about your current position so that you can plan your next steps. You have already internalized the necessary characteristics as a basis. Some may already be fully developed, others you may only have as seeds within you. Depending on whether you decide to develop these further, you will need to sow, water and nurture the seeds so that they grow into new traits. On the other hand, there may also be traits that you don't particularly like, but which you have very strongly developed. In this case, it is important to shape them with secateurs so that the small new plants are not overgrown. Your inner goal should be a diverse garden where you can relax in a deckchair without a second thought. What does the garden look like right now, at this very moment? Please take a few minutes to reflect on yourself and think very carefully about who you are. What makes up your personality? What makes you different from others?

To make it easier to understand, the pattern of behavior to be discarded is referred to as a "weed" and the desired pattern of behavior as a "rose", in line with the garden metaphor. The second step involves analyzing and communicating with pattern X in order to find out what causes this characteristic.

This is by no means easy and requires immense concentration, as this step presupposes that there is a trigger in the consciousness for each negative behavioral pattern that you can actively make contact with. Communication with the part that triggers the unloved "weed" behavior pattern can work in a variety of ways, including non-verbally, for example via sounds. The third step is to try to separate the "weed" behavior pattern from its trigger. One of the basic assumptions of neurolinguistic programming applies here, namely that every action, every action and therefore every action pattern is based on a positive intention.

This also applies to the part that triggers the "weed" pattern and disfigures our garden, ergo our personality. It is now increasingly a matter of communicating with this part and finding out why exactly it provokes the behavior pattern. If you think you have found a possible positive intention, you need to ask the part that is responsible for the weeds in our garden whether you are right in your assumption. If the answer to the question is "no", we need to find another motive, another positive intention. If the answer is "yes", we move on to the next step of the six-step reframing.

The fourth step involves finding alternatives to the undesirable "weed" behavior pattern. At best, some alternatives have already been anchored so that the part responsible for the pattern can, to a certain extent, look for alternative courses of action on its own.

At the beginning of the fifth step, you communicate with the trigger again and make sure that they are completely satisfied with the new alternatives and are prepared to take responsibility for them. This provides a kind of safeguard for the future and ensures that each of the three alternatives is finally recognized. It is now possible to check whether the new behaviors have been fully accepted - after all, in step two, we found out what triggers pattern X and what goal is being pursued with it. Conversely, this means that the expected reaction can just as easily be provoked. In contrast to the previous situation, however, the trigger of X now has three new options to choose from. This flexibility allows the triggering part to react to more stimuli. The sixth step is merely a kind of ecological check. Finally, not only the trigger of pattern X, but each of the inner parts of a person is asked whether they are satisfied with the new alternatives.

Swish technique
The swish technique helps to get rid of unwanted, annoying habits. However, this technique is best suited to people who have a strong visual imagination, as the negative trait in question and the positive trait with which it is to be replaced must be conjured up in the mind's eye. The standard Swish technique works with the three submodalities of size, distance and brightness. In principle, it is simply a matter of letting

the image of the visualized negative trait slide smaller, darker and further away until it is finally out of sight and the trait is thus discarded, and on the other hand, letting the image of the visualized positive trait get bigger, brighter and closer so that it properly replaces the negative habit.

Here too, the first step is to identify the negative habit you want to get rid of. For example, a stressful situation can trigger the impulse to smoke a cigarette because this is your learned response to stress.

In order to get into a new, more constructive habit in response to your stress, you need a substitute action that is as positive as possible, which ideally even helps you to cope with your stress in a better and healthier way and which also makes you feel good. For example, instead of smoking a cigarette, you could spend the same amount of time drinking a nice cup of tea instead. The positive effect of the cigarette is only an illusion and the reward effect only lasts as long as you smoke it. However, consciously drinking a cup of tea can offer you much more, you have a positive taste experience, which equates to an initial reward factor, and the actual physically calming effect of the drink provides a clearly noticeable and longer-lasting reward effect.

Since, as usual with neuro-linguistic programming, the principle that every reaction has a trigger also applies here, the second step is to ask what immediately precedes the unwanted habit and thus provokes it. As a rule, such a trigger is an emotion - usually a negative one, due to which the trait to be eliminated comes to light, in this case stress.

The third step involves visualizing the disruptive habit and visualizing the reaction that will replace the negative one. Many things are suitable for this. However, the most reliable method has proven to be to take your own reflection in the mirror, with facial expressions and gestures reflecting the respective characteristics as accurately as possible.

If you can see both visualizations as accurately as possible in your mind's eye, the actual swish begins in the fourth step. It is best to imagine a kind of screen, such as a large television or a screen. This screen is completely filled with the image of the negative trait, i.e. smoking a cigarette. In the bottom right-hand corner, the image of the positive habit, i.e. the tea ceremony, now appears, very dark and small at first. Paint this picture as clearly and in as much detail as possible so that you can taste and smell the tea and feel the relaxation setting in. Once you have achieved this, associate these feelings in your mind with a specific color, which you then place over the picture. This will now become bigger and brighter, gradually spreading from the bottom right-hand corner across the entire screen.

At the same time, the image of the negative habit becomes smaller and darker until it is finally completely overlaid by its positive counterpart and disappears altogether. The screen is now completely covered by the visualization of the desired positive trait. This completes the swish. In the fifth step, the standard swish is repeated seven times in the best case scenario. The sixth step is a test to see whether the swish was successful. All you have to do is try to visualize the negative characteristic again. If the swish was successful, this should actually be impossible. If the image appears, the standard swish must be repeated. Another way to determine the success of this method is to carry out a real test, i.e. to evoke the situation that preceded the unwanted habit and see whether it has been replaced by its positive counterpart.

Fast Phobia
This neuro-linguistic programming technique works with audio-visual creativity, which may be difficult

and complicated at first, but with sufficient concentration leads to sensational successes.

Using the fast phobia technique, phobias can be made to disappear at record speed, sustainably and permanently. Phobia patients cannot choose what they are afraid of, and when they are confronted with the relevant object, animal or similar, a movie automatically runs in their head that cannot be stopped and puts the person concerned into a kind of state of shock.

The fast phobia technique uses this film by playing a situation that is closely linked to the phobia as a black and white film in front of the inner eye. After a few steps, this is played back again in color. This should make the phobia disappear after several repetitions. In order to understand and, above all, apply this technique, you first need to be aware of what a phobia actually is and what causes it. The answer, at least to the latter, is simple: in your own head.

The mind is the origin of every phobic disorder. The interesting point is that even those affected know that a phobia is always irrational. It is directed against an object of any nature chosen by one's own mind, without drawing on the personal experience of the person concerned.

This means that you can suffer from aviophobia, the panic fear of flying in an airplane, without either ever having flown yourself or without having had any experiences that could be the cause of the phobia, despite having already flown. This is also the fundamental difference between a phobia and an anxiety disorder.

This is also a pathological form of anxiety that has almost the same symptoms as a phobia. However, in contrast to a phobic disorder, an anxiety disorder is actually based on a negative experience in relation to the object in question. This means that someone who has a panicky and explicitly non-phobic fear of flying suffers from it because they have actually almost crashed once, survived a crash or lost a loved one in a crash. At this point, it should be expressly mentioned that fast phobia only helps with phobias and not with anxiety disorders, which are much more severe because they are more traumatic. There are numerous ways to avoid the trigger for the symptoms of a phobia.

If you have a panic fear of elevators, you can avoid stairs - the phobia is only triggered when you approach the elevator with the intention of entering and using it. However, these avoidance methods only treat the symptoms, not the actual phobia. And this is where Fast Phobia comes into play.

Let's stay with the example of aviophobia - fear of flying - and come back to the movie mentioned at the beginning, which plays in the mind's eye. This is triggered as soon as the person concerned approaches an airplane, in some cases even as soon as they enter the airport, when the brain knows that the feared situation is imminent.

The start of the movie is the brain's signal that the minimum distance to the object of fear has been exceeded. The movie is played as a final, ultimate warning and contains exactly the worst-case scenario that one fears, and the body, as the sole viewer of the movie, reacts with the physical symptoms of a phobia - racing pulse, sweating, panic attacks, fainting.

From this perspective, it can be said that the body does not react in panic to the plane or the flight, but to the movie playing in the mind's eye. The key to combating a phobia therefore lies in controlling this movie - you have to learn to take control of it yourself. Incidentally, this movie does not only run in relation to the object of the phobia. In numerous potentially dangerous situations that do not inspire confidence, the brain warns us of impending disaster by means of a disaster movie. However, unlike phobics, humans are usually able to stop this movie and prevent the fear from arising in the first place.

The fast phobia technique aims to enable the person affected to gain sole control over the feared inner movie, to practically become their own director in order to overcome the fear in this way. This is achieved by means of two basic practices.

Firstly, you train yourself to view the film dissociated, i.e. separately and not as part of your own being, and to watch it in black and white instead of in color. Once the film has been played, the second practice is used to play the film in color and backwards, and in contrast to the black and white version, it is played back in association, i.e. as part of the self again. After regular use, the phobia should be conquered. If not, it may not actually be a phobia, but possibly an anxiety disorder, or the fear may have a completely different origin.

Why NLP is ideal for manipulation

You may already have a good idea of why NLP is well suited to manipulation. However, we would like to briefly go into this again. Remember: NLP comes from psychotherapy. When you get right down to it, psychotherapy can perhaps be considered the absolute king of manipulation, because who could be a more successful manipulator than a person who gets patients with pathological mental disorders to behave differently? People whose behaviors have often been burned deep into their own psyche by trauma and other bad events. They want to bring about change on a much more superficial level in people who are usually mentally healthy. Realizing this reveals the full potential of NLP.

In fact, even within the NLP scene, the question of how to protect oneself from using NLP too manipulatively arises time and again. Many of the techniques are aimed at highly manipulating other people from the outset. Those who use NLP therapeutically must therefore adhere to certain protocols to ensure that they do not harm their patients. Be aware of the power that NLP gives you over other people. Use the techniques described carefully and always question whether you are doing the other person a favor. Then there is nothing to stop you from using them.

Manipulation techniques

The responsibility that NLP entails has already been mentioned in an earlier chapter. Anyone who remembers these words may frown in surprise or even doubt and wonder how responsible use of NLP methods and the word manipulation can possibly go together.

This doubt is due to the mainly negative connotation of manipulation, which is generally understood as a negative form of influencing. As a rule, the actions, thoughts and/or feelings of the other person, the person being manipulated, are manipulated. It is always assumed - and this also explains the negative connotation - that the manipulator acts purely out of self-interest and - as mentioned at the beginning - consciously accepts possible harm to the manipulated person.

Another basic assumption that gives manipulation a rather bad reputation is that the manipulated person can only ever be influenced reluctantly and in a position that is adverse to them and therefore - which is the third basic assumption - resists the manipulation and must be "fought" in a psychological sense so that the negative influence is crowned with success. These are the prejudices against the concept of manipulation and they are highly questionable, as they are all based on the basic assumption that every person who consciously and purposefully exerts influence is acting out of selfish motives.

Out of selfishness, the manipulator tries to impose his opinion, his thinking, etc. on the manipulated person. This completely ignores the fact that everyone is manipulated almost every day - both consciously and unconsciously. Even supposedly simple things such as the body language already mentioned and deliberate modifications of this to create a consciously induced effect fall under the category of manipulation. Teachers manipulate their pupils in various and - contrary to the basic assumptions mentioned - harmless ways, and for managers in companies in particular, numerous manipulation options prove to be elementary in terms of successful personnel policy. In order to show that manipulation is far less harmful than its reputation suggests and to explain the useful aspects of conscious and unconscious influence, various manipulation techniques that everyone is capable of using are described below.

THE HANGING RECORD AKA THE REPETITION

One of the most common and - as the name suggests - most harmless forms of manipulation. We experience this aspect of deliberately influencing the actions and thoughts of others every day in advertising - hundreds of commercials are repeated several times from commercial break to commercial break. The background to all of this is that humans are creatures of habit - the more often they are regularly presented with something via their perception channels, the more natural the advertised object becomes for them, the more often they think of it and the more willing they are to buy the product in question.

THE INERTIA TRAP

This manipulation technique is also well known and very popular. It is also known as the "foot in the door" technique and will be familiar to the majority of readers, as most of them have fallen into this "trap" themselves. It is often used in all kinds of supermarkets, shopping centers or large specialist stores as well as in public places such as train stations or popular spots in city centers.

Pretty much everyone has, at some point in their lives, come across a stall offering newspapers, entries into generous and even too tempting competitions or simply a new range of certain food products that have appeared on the market. You are approached by friendly salespeople and asked if you would like to try one of the products described - free of charge, of course - and then you fall into the trap. If you show interest in the offer, the salesperson uses all his charm and tries his best to win over the customer in the long term.

THE FRIENDSHIP TRICK

This manipulation technique is ideal for breaking the ice with a stranger and can be used, for example, in the first few days at a new workplace to warm up to new colleagues. The friendship trick is based on a principle of communication that aims to emphasize as many similarities as possible between the conversation partners and is combined to a certain extent with the technique of repetition. An example conversation between two strangers:

Person A.: "I love going out to eat at restaurant XY. The food there is first class."

Person B (manipulator): "I've been there too, and I'm still amazed by the atmosphere today!"

Person A: "Oh, really? And what do you say to ..."

A conversation has already started between the two parties and person A gets the feeling that they are on the same wavelength as person B simply because they like the same restaurant - the ice is broken. However, the friendship trick is also often used by salespeople to suggest a feeling of familiarity and commonality to potential customers, which should ultimately lead to the sale of a particular product.

MANIPULATION BY CREATING FEAR

Anyone who wants to manipulate people by creating fear makes use of the rarely useful human characteristic of generally thinking subjectively and feeling irrationally. In a business meeting, for example, the manipulator prepares the audience for a period of time to generate fear by using particularly emotional content in the presentation, speech, etc. or by using a passionate delivery style.

Metaphorically speaking, this opens up an emotional channel for the listeners, who are now much more receptive to the creation of fear. This is ultimately caused, for example, by the darkest possible version of the company's future if certain changes desired by the manipulator are not implemented for the good of the company. The larger the group of listeners, the more fear each individual ultimately feels, through a kind of herd effect, which has also been responsible for many a mass panic.

HERD INSTINCT

This form of manipulation usually happens un-consciously and can also be observed in many work-places. It is based on the phenomenon that in many situations, an individual person always follows a group, a small group follows a large group, a large group follows an even larger group and so on. What a large group does is always perceived as correct by the next smaller group and imitated as a result. As with the friendship trick, the familiarization phase of a person in a new working environment also serves as an example here.

If you are used to a certain work routine or company philosophy from your previous employer and the new employer's seems completely contradictory and contrary to the old one, it won't be long before you have internalized the new work processes and, thanks to the approval of your work colleagues who are used to nothing else, will eventually approve of them. Your own opinions and convictions always adapt to those of the herd. It's frightening, but true.

EMOTIONAL TRICKS

Manipulation via feelings is quite easy, as our feelings do not appeal to our intellect. If our request cannot be implemented on a factual level, it may be possible to implement it via the emotional channel. This type of manipulation is used to limit or interrupt the other person's ability to criticize. The emotional trick is used, for example, with sad photos at fundraising galas.

How do you recognize the manipulation of others?

Am I being manipulated or not? That is the question here. Anyone who is familiar with manipulation techniques knows what is going on. Wherever you walk and stand, you manipulate: on the train, in the streetcar, in the restaurant, simply everywhere, and you do it with words, hands and facial features. These are the signals you send out, and so you are manipulated in return. In principle, you don't have to ask yourself whether you are being manipulated - you are.

Everyone tries to assert their interests and sell themselves well. But there is one manipulation technique that many do not have, namely self-confidence. But this is as important as butter on bread. There are professionals who always get what they want because they live by the **four-method manipulation principle**.

THE FOUR-METHOD MANIPULATION PRINCIPLE

1. They want to destroy your self-confidence: They only ever point out your mistakes and what you are specifically doing wrong. They just want to make you feel worse and worse.

2. They punish you with disregard and ignorance: if you need help, they try to keep you down. You are forced to follow their actions, otherwise you will not be helped.

3. They ignore reality and put forward crude theories: they spread fear in discussions and want to incite others. They themselves are happy when others tear each other apart and fight each other.

4. They keep your personality small: they feel stronger and want you to stay small. As long as you feel bad, you keep going and enjoy it.

WHAT IS BEHIND A MANIPULATIVE PERSONALITY?

Are you one of them or do you have to learn manipulation from scratch? We are manipulated every day, our actions and thoughts change and we don't even realize it. Probably not even the person who is manipulating. He imposes his will, nothing more. However, manipulation can certainly be a form of control if it is carried out knowingly. As a result, there are perpetrators and victims if the manipulation is not directional but purely negative.

There are more than enough manipulated victims. There are many people with a narcissistic personality disorder and such a personality is only too happy to bully those around them. These people are scary and constantly talk down to you. They are disrespectful and ungrateful, threatening and aggressive. These people are all of these things.

But if you are a person who manipulates others yourself, then you should never treat others in this way. It is more inhumane than humane. Nevertheless, these people get very far with their manipulation, as they are almost married to the word intimidation and have internalized the manipulative ways of acting. This behavior is almost comparable to that of a spider and its web: it wraps up its prey until it eventually feeds on it. In this way, these people rob you of the last of your energy. But if a person like you comes across this very manipulative person, the tide turns. You can also manipulate and you won't fall into this spider's web. Manipulation is a combination of politics, sociology and psychology.

And this is how manipulation works with these people, so beware: it's all about pure influence, which is exactly what makes people who almost suffer from a personality disorder. Influence is very often used as a synonymous term for manipulation. However, it lacks the aspect of targeted exploitation, which is the case with manipulation. In politics, one would speak of propaganda in this context.

In this way, the manipulation of politics serves to spread ideological ideas in order to influence public opinion. Emotional influence runs counter to our democratic principles, as we as human beings want to make free and autonomous decisions. We want to make decisions that arise from our reason and passion. Nevertheless, external influence can be part of this. We are simply manipulated. People who influence us in a purely negative way restrict us and make us feel small. Don't let these people scare you off and get out of their haze, because they pollute the air.

Principles of human communication

Even if you don't want to in some situations - you are always communicating, at all times and every second. If not via words, then via body language, i.e. gestures, facial expressions and overall articulation. The tricky thing about body language is that while - in most situations at least - you make conscious and controlled decisions about the words you say, the inexperienced user rarely has control over body language, which means that what you say can sometimes be quite absurd.

A person's gestures - and it doesn't matter whether they are clearly recognizable signs or so-called microgestures - reveal a great deal about the author and their character to the trained eye. Incredibility often arises, for example, when the articulation does not match what is being said. The image is not rounded and betrays dubious intentions. The spoken word is not always convincing. The majority of communication is non-verbal. Salespeople in particular use 90 percent non-verbal communication, because body language is their communication element. On the other hand, the harmony of words and body language conveys a feeling of high authenticity and credibility. It is therefore safe to say that body language plays a decisive, if not the decisive role in human communication.

Perhaps you have noticed that we use our ears more than our eyes in a conversation? Of course we listen carefully, but what we say and our posture don't always match. The body does not lie in the way it expresses itself and cannot hide or conceal many things. We express ourselves more intensively with our body language than with our voice. As a result, our posture betrays our thoughts, because we cannot hide behind it so easily. For example, we only use the pitch of our voice 38 percent of the time and only 7 percent of the time in the rest of our communication. The big picture comes from body language. Those who are successful in both business and private life always present themselves holistically. If we take a few steps back in our lives, babies communicate through sounds, but also a great deal through gestures and facial expressions. This allows us as parents or grandparents to interpret how they are feeling.

We understand each other practically without words. The first step is therefore non-verbal communication, which is the final coding. We communicate through our posture, facial expressions and gestures, then we use words. In some ways, this happens completely unconsciously and is a big part of us. A mouthpiece in a class of its own. We come across as more authentic and honest than with words. We do not disguise ourselves in body language. It usually occurs spontaneously as a result of a reaction. This makes us appear more genuine and emotional.

The fascinating thing about body language, however, is that it not only influences the external image of one's own character - with an appropriately self-confident appearance, the self-image can also be changed for the better. It is not for nothing that many motivational coaches start with the body language of their clients, as this can have an amazing influence on character when developed positively. The first and most important step in this direction is to understand that, in most cases, body language happens completely unconsciously and can only be used if you start to make conscious use of it. With enough practice, every gesture will be exactly as it should be, from the slightest movement of the fingers to the play of the eyebrows - and the desired effects can be achieved with the other person.

Anyone who works intensively with body language can claim to be a person with talented abilities. It also allows you to penetrate deep into the other person's psyche. A glance is often enough, because gestures and facial expressions work very well together. Before you even say a word, the person who has mastered body language knows who they are dealing with. So be attentive and don't let the words put you off, the body is more likely to speak the truth. The effect of body language is therefore phenomenal and unique and should be emphasized much more.

One of the most important indicators of body language is not gestures - it can be found in the human eyes. These are not only used for identification - it is well known that every person has a unique pair of eyes

- but by reading the eyes, you can also draw astonishing conclusions about the character and mood of their owner. Intensive eye contact can be a particularly pleasant or a particularly unpleasant experience, depending on who you are making it with, even though you are basically doing nothing more than looking at each other. This is because the eyes - to use a well-known saying - are the window to the soul and you feel at the mercy of particularly prolonged eye contact. When it comes to first impressions, most people are guided by the eyes (and general facial expressions) of the other person; both consciously and unconsciously, conclusions are drawn about character from eye and facial expressions. These are not new, spectacular findings from any university or the latest developments in human behavior - on the contrary. Homo sapiens have been reading the eyes of their fellow human beings and trying to identify emerging intentions and feelings in them for as long as we have existed.

The question remains: what exactly can you recognize in these unique and often mysterious eyes? Particularly strong, obvious emotions are the easiest to recognize. Joy, anger or fear are difficult to conceal and can be read in the eyes even with a high degree of self-control. This is simply because the expression in the eyes is largely the result of contractions of the inner eye muscles, which are provoked directly by the autonomic nervous system and therefore cannot be consciously controlled - similar to your own heartbeat, for example. The pupil, or rather its size, is particularly revealing. This not only depends on the prevailing incidence of light - it is known that the pupil enlarges in dark light conditions, whereas it is contracted by the iris muscles in bright light. We can also notice dilated pupils in our counterparts in anxiety states, for example. This is because when we feel anxious, our brain automatically feels the need to pay attention and, by enlarging the pupil, ensures an increased incidence of light and thus a better perception of our surroundings. However, the main condition for interacting with other people is that there are generally people available to interact with. This is the case for most people.

Everyone has social contacts, family and a circle of friends. Loneliness is not at all good for most people - quite a few researchers would say "everyone" at this point. The mere thought of being alone, if you think it through to its logical conclusion, conjures up feelings of unease and a gloomy mood. In some life situations, however, loneliness is temporarily unavoidable. How do people manage to cope with this and why are social contacts so important to them? It is no secret that the human need for friends and social interaction is evolutionary. After all, prehistoric man was best able to survive in a pack, where he was best armed against attacks from outside and was able to ensure that living conditions improved steadily over time. This idea is so deeply rooted in his DNA that he has not been able to shake it off to this day. In situations where we cannot avoid temporary loneliness, we become very aware of this. For example, if you change your place of residence, employer or leave your parents' home for the first time, the settling-in phase is usually difficult due to a lack of social contacts.

Further proof of the importance of a circle of friends is provided by the entertainment industry - or rather the film and series industry. It is certainly no coincidence, for example, that the most successful sitcoms of recent years, from "Friends" to "How I Met Your Mother" or "Big Bang Theory", are all about different friends living together. These series offer no particular drama, no action or wild chases. Basically, we just watch our best friends getting their - admittedly quite weird and unusual - everyday lives together.

The message of this series is the same in almost every episode - friendship is the most important thing in life. When Ted Mosby is once again unsuccessful with women and sits dejected in his apartment, his friends are always there for him. They support each other, laugh and cry together.

Together - this is the big secret, both for the success of the series in question and for everyday life. If you scientifically compare two people, one of whom is happy in life and the other unhappy, then in several cases the happiness will be due to the presence of social contacts and the unhappiness to the lack of them. If you have people in your life with whom you can share it, with whom you can share the joyful as well as the sad and devastating moments, your view of your own identity, your own existence, is much more optimistic and full of life than if you have to live through all the situations that life in all its diversity has in store for you alone.

But loneliness doesn't just make people unhappy. In certain cases, a permanent lack of social contact can even lead to physical illness. This is particularly the case if the social environment is not exactly conducive to jumping for joy. If a person's social environment is dreary, gloomy and joyless, this automatically has an effect on their own psyche. Although this does not necessarily mean that a negative environment produces a negative person, it can reinforce already latent, pessimistic predispositions and intensify a depressive mood and solidify it in the core of the character. On the other hand, a positive environment rarely has a negative effect on a person and, just like negative circumstances, can have an impact on already latent character traits and basic attitudes.

Interpreting the unconscious signals of our body

In a conversation, an argument or in our emotional world, unconscious gestures arise. They emerge almost reflexively. It is not just a reaction to a certain thing, it is an honest feeling. We express it immediately and without thinking.

These unconscious signals often arise when we receive bad news. We react immediately and usually without any control over ourselves. This is also the case with happy surprises, but also occurs with tension and fear. Our body thus communicates unconsciously.

Eye movement patterns

The movements of the eyes can provide information about how the mental processes in the person's brain are probably taking place. Nevertheless, it should be emphasized that it is not advisable to come to a conclusion too quickly and thus make a hasty decision.

The construction of thought processes and the recollection of what has already been experienced is not a simple process, the truthful answer to which lies exclusively with the person in question. It should also be noted that a sequence of eye movements and thus eye movement patterns can usually be observed. This is due to the fact that every person goes through a variety of thought processes and therefore different eye movement patterns can be recognized. Finally, it should be noted that the following illustrations of eye movement patterns are generally aimed at right-handed people.

If you or the person you are talking to is left-handed, you may need to turn the explanations around, as the eye movements are then often reversed.

In the following, a distinction is made between eye movements upwards and downwards as well as to the left and to the right, still in the horizontal or in the horizontal plane or centered.

If your counterpart's eyes are directed **upwards,** you can assume that the person prefers the visual representation system for receiving information. If the gaze is then directed **upwards to the left, it can be** said that the visually represented information is remembered information. This means that your counterpart probably sees situations in his or her mind's eye that he or she has experienced before. In other words, the person then recalls familiar images.

To test this on a person of your choice, you could, for example, ask what color your parents' kitchen is, or how a friend's or acquaintance's room is furnished.

On the other hand, the eye movement to the **top right** shows that your counterpart visualizes things and situations, but he or she does not remember this representation, but **constructs** it. This means that visualizations of this kind have never happened before or that the person has never seen them with their own eyes. It is possible that you can deduce from this which of the two forms of memory a person uses. This will then help you to align and optimize your communication accordingly.

Having already explained the upward eye movements, it seems appropriate to now examine the eye movement patterns that are directed **downwards.** The movement patterns of this type cannot be assigned to a preferred representation system overall. However, a distinction is again made as to whether the gaze is directed **downwards and to the right** or **downwards and to the left**.

Eye movement patterns that occur more frequently towards **the bottom left** show that your interaction partner is **conducting an inner dialog with themselves**. This process of inner dialog often takes place on an auditory level. This means that when your partner looks to the bottom left, he or she is usually talking to themselves in order to discuss something with themselves. Through the inner dialog, he or she is trying to come to terms and find a solution.

However, if your interaction partner's eyes are directed to **the bottom right,** this can be clearly assigned to the kinaesthetic representation system. This means that kinaesthetic processes are taking place in this person's head during his or her thoughts. The other person is feeling something or is **emotionally involved**. It is also possible that the other person is evoking a feeling.

The conscious sig-
nals of our body

Yes, we also have trained skills. These are expressed with a targeted look, a confident handshake and the well-known poker face. This allows everyone to draw conclusions without words. We know this from self-observation, gestures and observation. Conscious signals are always targeted and aim to elicit a reaction or an intention, whether at a job interview, a dismissal or at a conference. Face to face in a non-verbal version - this is how business is done in professional life. It's just important not to let the body's signals hang too far out of the window, otherwise we mercilessly expose our feelings and thoughts. A trained observer can read us better than we would like. That's why it's important never to let anyone look at your cards during negotiations or arguments. Present yourself professionally and with full physical commitment.

THE GOLDEN RULES OF BODY LANGUAGE

No matter where we are, non-verbal communication accompanies us wherever we go and wherever we stand. Sometimes it expresses the opposite of what we say. That's why it takes center stage and is more important than we think. We send signals and express ourselves without words. Below you can read the golden rules for better non-verbal communication that can help you succeed.

Poor

What do arms have to say in which position and posture? Crossing your arms in front of your chest tends to signal a defensive protective or defensive posture. They therefore stand out as a barrier. If, on the other hand, you cross your arms behind your head or your hands are clasped behind your neck and your elbows are deliberately stretched outwards, this means something like "I am the leader of the pack and am brimming with self-confidence". Then there is another variant of the elbows, because if they are pointing towards the person you are talking to, this means nothing other than that they should not come too close.

Eye contact

Looking relaxed and not staring, but still keeping a close eye on the person you are talking to - that is what non-verbal communication is all about. However, it is important to be able to look the other person in the eye. Otherwise you will appear insecure and self-conscious.

Distance

Don't get on anyone's nerves and give yourself and others the space bubble. We all live with it unconsciously. Otherwise we are invading each other's personal space. The rule of thumb is: an outstretched arm's length is enough and provides the necessary individual distance. Too much closeness is met with defensive behavior.

Handshake

The first physical contact between two people is not a kiss, no, in business it is a handshake. It is not banal, because it says more than a thousand words. It sounds so simple, but it's not. How do I shake hands properly without appearing clumsy or insecure? It's important to find the happy medium, a short, firm squeeze and not too long, please. You don't want to warm each other's hands. Don't grab the whole hand, just the front part up to the fingers and don't forget to shake it three times. And not with an exuberant temperament.

Hands

You can quickly tell who you are dealing with by looking at their hands. An open person does not close their hands. Their fingers are not interlocked because the person is open to conversation and new things. If, on the other hand, the hands are closed, the non-verbal weapons kick in, which in turn indicates defensive behavior. If someone is thinking, the fingertips of both hands gently nestle together.

Posture

Don't walk into a room hunched over, walk straight. This should not come across as arrogant, it shows a certain presence. The posture demonstrates stability and brings self-confidence. Remain calm and composed and do not make any hectic or excited gestures. A calm demeanor has a calming effect.

Smile

When you enter a room - this could be at a meeting or a presentation - start by positioning yourself. Smile in a relaxed manner and let everything sink in for a moment. A smile is convincing and encourages others to like you.

Body language and NLP

The important concept of neurolinguistic programming brings about change and the associated communication. Neurolinguistics: The brain and language serve as an effective tool and are closely linked to body language. This is how people react, as we basically long for a guidance system. Everyone needs a "guide wolf" and so do you. Based on the information available, a person functions almost perfectly and makes the right decisions.

SYMPATHY

You can get far with sympathy, doors and gates are o-pen to you and this is exactly what you should take advantage of when manipulating. These rules are worth their weight in gold and let the manipulation work for you, because if you gain their trust, they won't find the manipulation unpleasant. On the contrary, they will feel flattered.

The golden rules of sympathy
Rule no. 1 Maintain eye contact without staring and smile skillfully. This in turn conveys openness.
Rule no. 2 Signal your attention to discreetly adopt the other person's body language. This could be under-stood by the other person as: "I am like you, I listen to you and believe you."
Rule no. 3 Regularly call your conversation partner by their first name, because let's be honest: we love to hear our name. You do too.
Rule no. 4 Always give an honest opinion and lead by example in our society.
Rule no. 5 Be polite and friendly, offer drinks and make small talk. This will certainly take the tension and nervousness out of the (new) situation.

Rule #6 Empathy, or compassion, and the ability to put yourself in someone else's shoes and emotions, builds a lot of trust.

Rule no. 7 Look for things you have in common. These can be interests and hobbies, which can also help to build trust.

The power of the psyche

It often starts with an innocent smile and then the manipulation takes its course. We are subject to many mechanisms, starting with our feelings, thoughts, emotions and behavior. Are you a person who is ambitious and knows what they want? Then your psyche is strong, you are balanced and decisive. Not everyone can claim this, but you are one of them. You can manipulate people and make use of your own likeability, your sympathy, which immediately puts the other person in a positive mood. This is your instinct and your psyche guides you. Your psyche works hand in hand with you and you skillfully work out some manipulation strategies. But how do you get others to do what you want? Quite simply: with manipulation. Even praise alone can be a hidden manipulation. You tell your employee that you only see them behind the project. He feels flattered and gets started immediately. In reality, you want the project to be completed as quickly as possible.

Did you know that even sulking is a manipulation strategy? It is, and it doesn't just bring with it a negative feeling, because sulking also wants to achieve something. Children are quite good at it and even adults have not forgotten how to sulk. The following therefore applies: anyone who sulks has something to say to you in disguise and you certainly won't fall for this emotional trick. On the one hand we manipulate, on the other we communicate. Sometimes it is a covert battle using unfair means. But the one who expresses the most persuasive power wins. Think very carefully about how you proceed in life and what means you use to win. Manipulation has the same power as your psyche, because you are primarily guided and controlled by it. Our psyche can feel, think, perceive and make a self-fulfilling prophecy. It reflects our behavior.

Whether information, complex events or individual stimuli, your on-board computer has everything neatly stored. It also learns to make friends with the manipulation. The brain perceives and emotional effects take place. You need to have a firm grip on your psyche when you manipulate, and some tactics require nerves of steel. With your keen perception, you can better assess your surroundings, read people and evaluate them optimally. This is precisely the skill you possess. These advantages are very useful in both your business and private life.

This is where another helper of your psyche comes in: feeling. Feelings and sensations are the guideposts in your life. Did you know that we felt before we could think? It began in the womb and this feeling is like a primal instinct. It is our guide and indicates our needs: Hunger, thirst, sleep, warmth, love, security and affection. Our basic trust has grown with us. If you have a strong personality, you have an emotional buffer at your disposal. This in turn is used in manipulation and, like a smile, can open doors for you. Anyone who uses manipulation for themselves must be at one with their psyche. This is why the topic has been included in this book. People with an unstable background will never see manipulation as a tool of power.

It tends to frighten them, they avoid these purely human abilities and are more likely to allow themselves to be manipulated than to see manipulation as a means to an end. Our world of thoughts is therefore our property; we are reluctant to let anyone look into our emotional world.

Anyone who manipulates has locked these anyway and acts purely effectively, speculatively and also manipulatively. Much of this, such as feeling, is part of our evolutionary roots and these also express our wishes, desires and needs. But you have all these evolutionary traits under control without batting an eyelid. As you can see, our brain performs a workload that should not be underestimated, day after day. Everything is stored and can be called up at any time. If we then take manipulation into our own hands, we can control people without them perceiving this as manipulation. That alone is your skillful advantage and an ability in itself.

In turn, our behavior, which includes acting or not acting as a behavioral pattern, puts the crown on our personality. We make contact with our behavior and with the outside world. We communicate, exchange opinions and interests and are communicative at all times. Our brain, i.e. the power of thought, is also subject to the reward system, which is associated with the neurotransmitter dopamine. Our happiness hormone is known to make us happy and joyful. It is precisely this buffer that we need in order to concentrate on our work and perform well.

Manipulation also needs a part of it. You want to act as a likeable person in order to call success your own. This hormone release is therefore a benefit for you and you turn the purely natural event to your advantage. Accordingly, we live with the fear center, the emotional protagonists and the reward system and this represents our behavioral pattern. We do not always act according to our free will, not even when we are manipulated, but we submit to our thoughts and our behavioral pattern. As you can see, manipulation can only do one part of the job; the rest is done by the psyche, because it has power over us.

Bonus material: Mindset diary

Now that you have learned the basics of positive thinking in detail, you will find instructions and tasks on how to put this knowledge into practice on the following pages.

The mindset diary also offers you an opportunity to express yourself creatively and give free rein to your thoughts on a non-judgmental piece of paper - so that you can then consider and evaluate them. Put what you have learned into practice straight away and change yourself and your mindset for the better!

MINDSET DIARY

More happiness in 14 days: This chapter is about setting aside a certain amount of time each day for yourself and completing various tasks or using thought-provoking ideas. First read through the task and then take up to 30 minutes to complete it.

Then write down in your mindset diary what your experience was. The aim is to fill at least three pages with your thoughts every day over a period of at least 14 days. You can either let your thoughts flow freely onto the pages or use the suggested tasks as a guide. Make it dependent on your mood on the day. Sometimes our mind just wants to get rid of ballast, sometimes it is happy to be given a new thought-provoking impulse. Many of the suggestions on the following pages may surprise you with their simplicity. But the more consistently you practise the suggested rituals and then reflect on them in your personal diary, the more clearly you will notice the progress. It is often the small pleasures that you overlook or even subconsciously deny yourself in the rush of everyday life.

Day 1: Be PRESENT in the here and now (meditation)

Take 15 to 30 minutes to meditate and then make an entry in your diary. What thoughts did you let pass during the meditation? Where did they come from? How did it feel not to give them any importance?

Day 2: Poster with your comfort zone

Draw a circle on an A3 poster. Write in the circle the things that you like to do and that make you feel good. Then write things around the circle that are outside your comfort zone. The further they are from the center, the less you feel comfortable doing them. This task can only work if you are honest with yourself. If you have completed the poster conscientiously, this overview will provide you with a clear guide to the things you can achieve in the coming months and years. Work your way from the center of your comfort zone to the edges step by step by doing exactly these things.

Day 3: A mind map ...

... your character traits. Think about this question: What makes you brilliant? Create another poster or write down in your diary in large letters what your particular strengths are. Every time you look at these posters, your subconscious will be reminded of all the things you can do. This ensures that negative thoughts and self-doubt no longer have a place.

Day 4: Personal wellbeing rituals

Introduce rituals that make you feel good in your own skin - even if it's just a few blissful, unobserved moments. This time for you counts. It might be your favorite song that you dance to at full volume, or fifteen minutes every day with one of the award-winning books you've always wanted to read. Maybe it's also time to do "nothing" in peace (if that's even possible with the human brain in an untrained state). Indulge your senses. Light some candles or a diffuser with essential oils. Incense sticks can also work wonders.

Day 5: Ground yourself

Spend time in nature. Ground yourself. Do some gardening or go for a walk with the dogs or family and friends. We live so much in our thoughts that we often forget the connection to the world around us. Remind yourself that you are a part of it.

Day 6: Actively practicing gratitude

Take a moment to be still, simply breathe in and enjoy your surroundings, preferably on a patch of grass. Now please close your eyes and take 1 to 2 deep breaths. Be aware of the feeling of gratitude for being alive. Be grateful for all the individuals around you, after all, they are all an expression of love in this world - just like you.

Day 7: Mindfulness meditation

Plan at least 15, but preferably 30 minutes today to do a mindfulness meditation. Make yourself comfortable in your favorite place to meditate and increase your mindfulness and awareness. How do you feel in this second, right now? Why? What can you change or do better?

Day 8: Show compassion for yourself and others

Be gentle with yourself (and as a result with others). Show understanding and compassion towards yourself. Don't be so hard on yourself. For example, pour yourself a coffee in the morning and sit in the sun. You will see what a difference it makes to the course of your day if you allow yourself a few minutes time out every day.

Day 9: Actively practicing self-love

Give yourself a little more love than usual today. Tidy up, take a hot bath or put on a nice outfit. Clean your home. Make yourself comfortable in the evening. An important aspect of self-love is getting enough rest and relaxation. Get enough sleep. Sometimes we don't even notice how we exhaust ourselves - even with un-healthy thoughts alone. Give your body the rest it needs. The hours of sleep required for recovery vary from person to person and also depend on your current life situation. So please don't worry if you haven't set your alarm clock on a day off work and continue to sleep peacefully for a few more hours. You obviously needed it in this case.

Day 10: Don't think, do

Get active and get out of your OWN HEAD. Pay special attention to your usual duties today. Weed, feed your pets or have a chat with an elderly person in the neigh-borhood.

Day 11: Time to be and for creativity

Take time for yourself. Stay away from the soul-de-stroying, bottomless pit that social media can be when you're feeling down. You should only allow this media to work for you, never against you. Get creative. For example, if you had a particularly emotional dream or intense encounter, let that spark of energy you're fee-ling guide your hand - whether it was a good experi-ence or a bad one. (In fact, negative energy can some-times be a greater creative catalyst than peace-joy-eggcake energy). Our dreams are essentially just creative stories that our subconscious mind makes up. Pick up a paintbrush or pen and paper. Transform your sensations into a manifestation of your depth and creativity.

Day 12: Music heals the soul
Play your favorite songs. Let the music soothe your soul. Sing your heart out and dance as freely as if you were all alone in the world. You can also create a playlist of your favorite songs from each episode of your life. Or perhaps you have an old CD or record that you haven't played for years. Music goes straight to your soul. Let it heal and carry you.

Day 13: Beautify your home
Decorate and design your home today. Pick some pretty flowers outside or buy a sunflower to brighten up your space. This will serve to create a living environment that perfectly supports you in fulfilling your individual needs. What do you really need to feel like a whole person? Is it a garden where you can dig around and plant vegetables and flowers? Or an art studio; a place with lots of light, fresh air and space; what kind of colors do you like; do you like wooden furniture or maybe a solid, soft bed that you can sink into at night? You deserve a place where you can

develop your full potential. This doesn't mean that the design has to cost a lot, not at all. Your home should just meet your individual needs and requirements for a warm, welcoming home.

Day 14: Thank yourself for your dedication
Congratulations! You have completed the fourteen-day program with commitment and perseverance.

Questions that you can answer in your diary today: What did you find particularly difficult over the 14 days and how did you overcome the hurdle? In which area have you grown the most as a result of the training? Which newly learned or strengthened skills are you particularly proud of? What was your best experience in the past two weeks? If you wish, you can keep up the daily writing routine that you have so carefully maintained over the past two weeks. The longer you spend with your inner self, the better you will get to know yourself. And that is the basis for your own personal happiness and long-term satisfaction and fulfillment. I wish you continued enjoyment on your journey and all the happiness in the world.

www.ingramcontent.com/pod-product-compliance
Lightning Source LLC
Chambersburg PA
CBHW051758130726

47987CB00003B/1019